ANIMALS *in* DANGER

Polar Bear

Rod Theodorou

Heinemann LIBRARY

www.heinemann.co.uk
Visit our website to find out more information about **Heinemann Library** books.

To order:
☎ Phone 44 (0) 1865 888066
▤ Send a fax to 44 (0) 1865 314091
▭ Visit the Heinemann Bookshop at www.heinemann.co.uk to browse our catalogue and order online.

First published in Great Britain by Heinemann Library, Halley Court, Jordan Hill, Oxford OX2 8EJ, a division of Reed Educational and Professional Publishing Ltd.
Heinemann is a registered trademark of Reed Educational & Professional Publishing Limited.

OXFORD MELBOURNE AUCKLAND JOHANNESBURG BLANTYRE
GABORONE IBADAN PORTSMOUTH NH (USA) CHICAGO

Designed by Ron Kamen
Illustrations by Dewi Morris/Robert Sydenham
Originated by Ambassador Litho Ltd.
Printed in Hong Kong/China

ISBN 0431 00139 1
05 04 03 02 01
10 9 8 7 6 5 4 3 2 1

British Library Cataloguing in Publication Data
Theodorou, Rod
  Polar Bear. - (Animals in Danger)
  1.Polar Bear - Juvenile literature 2.Endangered species - Juvenile literature
  I.Title
  599.7'86

Acknowledgements
The Publishers would like to thank the following for permission to reproduce photographs: B & C Alexander: p15; Ardea: Francois Gohier p20, Martin W Grosnick p4, M Watson p26; Associated Press: p24; Bat Conservation International: Merlin D Tuttle p4; BBC: Doug Allan pp9, 14, Jeff Foott pp5, 8, 25, Martha Holmes p18, Thomas D Mangelsen pp16, 21; Bruce Coleman: Johnny Johnson p6, Dr Scott Nielsen p7, John Shaw p4, Tom Schandy p11; FLPA: F Polking p13; NHPA: p12, Andy Rouse p17; Oxford Scientific Films: Norbert Rosing p27; Skishoot-Offshoot: p23; Still Pictures: B & C Alexander p22; WWF Photolibrary: Eric Dragesco p19.

Cover photograph reproduced with permission of BBC Natural History Unit.

Our thanks to Henning Dräger at WWF-UK for his comments in the preparation of this book.

Every effort has been made to contact copyright holders of any material reproduced in this book. Any omissions will be rectified in subsequent printings if notice is given to the Publisher.

Contents

Any words appearing in the text in bold, **like this**, are explained in the Glossary.

Animals in danger

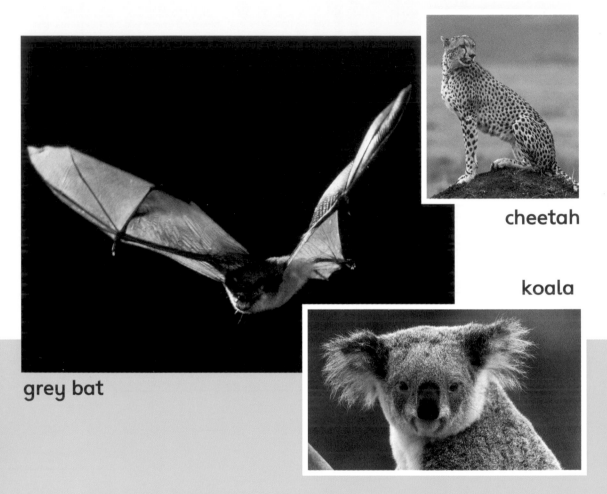

cheetah

koala

grey bat

All over the world, more than 25,000 animal **species** are in danger. Some are in danger because their home is being **destroyed**. Many are in danger because people hunt them.

This book is about polar bears and why they are in danger. Unless people learn to look after them, polar bears will become **extinct**. We will only be able to find out about them from books like this.

What are polar bears?

Polar bears are **mammals**. They are the largest member of the bear family. They are also the largest **carnivores** in the world that live on land!

Polar bears are very good swimmers and spend a lot of time in the sea. They can also run fast. They dig holes in the snow to shelter from the cold wind.

What do polar bears look like?

Polar bears have a narrower head and longer nose than other bears. They also have smaller ears and are covered in white fur.

Polar bears have very large, wide paws that act like snowshoes. They have fur underneath their paws to keep them warm and to stop them slipping on ice.

Where do polar bears live?

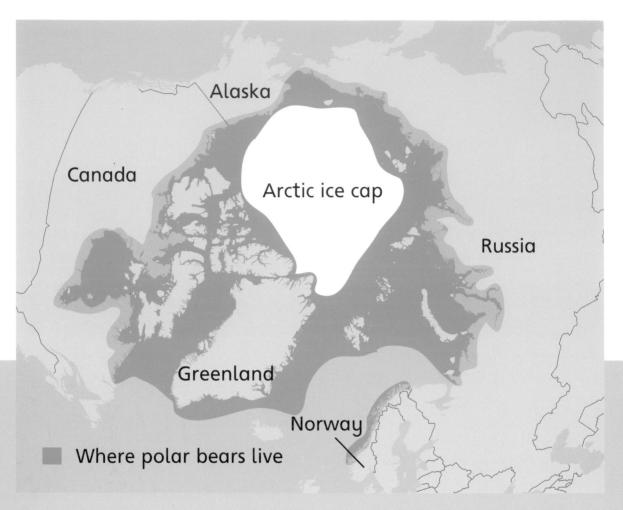

Alaska

Canada

Arctic ice cap

Russia

Greenland

Norway

Where polar bears live

Polar bears live on the frozen Arctic ice cap. They can also be found in Canada, Alaska, Greenland, northern Russia and on islands near Norway.

Polar bears like to live near the coast, or out on the **sea-ice** where they can hunt their **prey**. They like to keep on the move, and they travel great distances every year.

What do polar bears eat?

Polar bears are **carnivores**. Their favourite **prey** is the ringed seal. A polar bear will dig into the ice or lie for hours near a **blow-hole**, waiting to grab a seal with its sharp teeth and claws.

Polar bears will also attack young walrus. If they are very hungry they will hunt smaller prey like seabirds and fish. Sometimes they even eat plants or **forage** on rubbish tips.

Polar bear cubs

When a **female** polar bear is **pregnant** she digs a large **den** in the ice. Inside the den it is much warmer. Here she gives birth to one or two cubs.

The cubs are born around December. They are blind and only about 30 centimetres long. The mother feeds them her rich milk and they grow. Soon they are big enough to leave the den.

Looking after the cubs

In March the **female** comes out of the **den**. The cubs now weigh about 15 kilograms. They stay close to their mother as she leads them towards the coast to hunt.

The cubs watch how their mother hunts seals.
After two and a half years the mother leaves
her cubs. They are now big enough to hunt
for themselves.

Unusual polar bear facts

Polar bear fur is so thick and warm that the bears can overheat! Sometimes they take a swim in freezing icy water just to cool down.

Male polar bears are much bigger than **females**. Sometimes the males have 'play fights'. They both stand up and try to push each other over.

How many polar bears are there?

Thousands of years ago there were many more polar bears than there are today. In 1972 there were as few as 8500 polar bears left. The polar bear was close to becoming **extinct**.

The good news is that today there are about 24,000 polar bears alive. It is still very important that we help to **protect** bears for the future.

21

Why is the polar bear in danger?

Polar bears are so big and strong that they have no natural enemies. For thousands of years, humans have hunted polar bears for their thick warm fur.

In the 1950s and 1960s, people started to hunt polar bears with snowmobiles and aeroplanes. The polar bears had nowhere to hide and thousands were killed.

Why is the polar bear in danger?

Oil **exploration** in the Arctic has harmed the polar bear. Oil spills poison the seals which the bears eat. Oil also ruins the polar bear's fur.

Polar bears need large areas of ice to live on. **Global warming** means that the ice is slowly melting. This is very bad for the bears. Pollution on the ground, or in the air, is also a **threat**.

How is the polar bear being helped?

In 1973 the countries around the Arctic agreed to make the polar bear a **protected** species. They stopped most of the hunting. Now tourists hunt for polar bears – but only to take photographs!

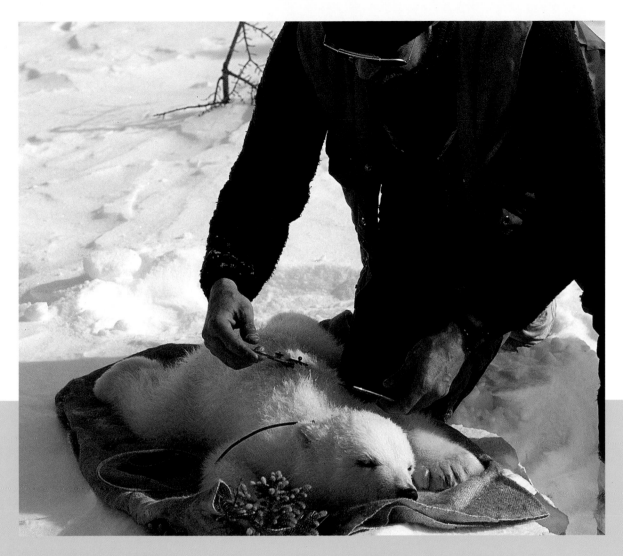

Conservation groups such as WWF (World Wide Fund for Nature) are working to stop illegal hunting and save the polar bear.

Polar bear factfile

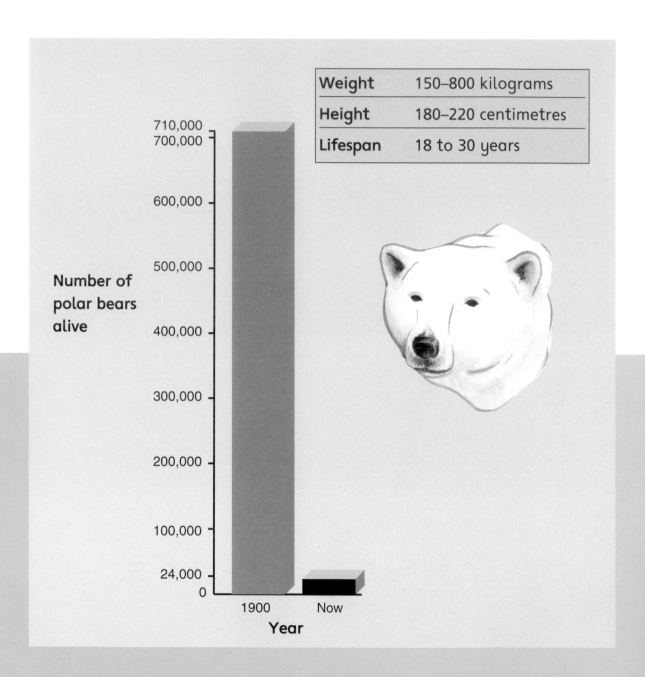

Weight	150–800 kilograms
Height	180–220 centimetres
Lifespan	18 to 30 years

Number of polar bears alive

710,000
700,000
600,000
500,000
400,000
300,000
200,000
100,000
24,000
0

1900   Now

Year

World danger table

	Number that may have been alive 100 years ago	Number that may be alive today
Cheetah	135,000	15,000
Grey bat	6.3 million	900,000
Koala	2 million	65,000
Leatherback turtle	1 million females	39,000 females
Whooping crane	2100	400

There are thousands of other animals in the world that are in danger of becoming **extinct**. This table shows some of these animals.

Can you find out more about them? yes,

29

Further reading, addresses and websites

Books

Amazing Bears, Amazing Worlds series, Theresa Greenaway, Dorling Kindersley, 1992

Polar Bear, Project Wildlife, Michael Bright, Aladdin Books, 1989

Polar Bears, Jump!, Ian Redmond, Dorling Kindersley, 1995

Polar Star, Sally Grindley and John Butler, Orchard Books, 1997

The Polar Bear on the Ice, Animal Habitats series, Martin Banks, Belitha Press, 1989

Vanishing Species, Miles Barton, Green Issues series, Franklin Watts, 1997

Organizations

Friends of the Earth: UK - 26–28 Underwood Street, London N1 7JQ ☎ (020) 7490 1555
Australia - 312 Smith Street, Collingwood, VIC 3065 ☎ 03 9419 8700

Greenpeace: UK - Canonbury Villas, London N1 2PN ☎ (020) 7865 8100
Australia - Level 4, 39 Liverpool Street, Sydney, NSW 2000 ☎ 02 9261 4666

WWF: UK - Panda House, Weyside Park, Catteshall Lane, Godalming, Surrey GU7 1XR ☎ (01483) 426444
Australia - Level 5, 725 George Street, Sydney, NSW 2000 ☎ 02 9281 5515

Useful websites

www.fws.gov
The US Fish and Wildlife Service site contains a polar bear fact sheet.

www.polarbearsalive.org
An organization dedicated to saving the polar bear.

www.sandiegozoo.org
The world famous American San Diego Zoo's site. Go to the Pick an Animal section for games and fact sheets.

www.seaworld.org
A fantastic site with lots of polar bear features.

www.wwf.org
WWF (World Wide Fund For Nature) is the world's largest independent conservation organization. WWF conserves wildlife and the natural environment for present and future generations.

Glossary

blow-hole	hole in the ice where seals come up to breathe air
carnivore	an animal that eats meat
conservation	looking after things, especially if they are in danger
den	safe place where animals can sleep or rest
destroyed	spoilt, broken or torn apart so it can't be used
exploration	visiting a place to find out what is there
extinct	dead and can never live again
female	girl or woman
forage	to try to find food
global warming	Earth slowly becoming hotter
male	boy or man
mammal	animal with hair like a human or a dog. Mammals drink their mother's milk as a baby.
pregnant	when a female animal is going to have a baby
prey	animals that are hunted and killed by other animals
protect	to look after. Some animals are protected by law.
sea-ice	ice that floats on the sea
species	a group of the same animals or plants
threat	when something is in danger from something else

31

Index

Titles in the *Animals in Danger* series include:

Hardback   0 431 00136 7

Hardback   0 431 00139 1

Hardback   0 431 00140 5

Hardback   0 431 00141 3

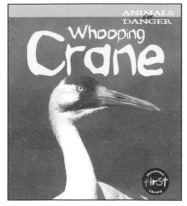

Hardback   0 431 00142 1

Hardback   0 431 00143 X

Find out about other Heinemann books on our website www.heinemann.co.uk/library